Cut & Copy

Creative ClipArt for...

PRIMARY

Original Designs by Dianne J. Hook

Deseret Book Company
Salt Lake City, Utah

With LOTS of love to Rachel:
Believe in yourself 'cause I sure do—and so does Heavenly Father.

Do you ever need a clever art idea for a handout at church—a note for visiting teaching or a handy calendar with some creative touches that you can quickly "copy off"? Then you'll love my new CUT & COPY clip art books! This series of easy-to-use books is designed especially with you in mind—the person in a hurry who wants to enhance your projects with fun art work. Combine these illustrations to create the desired effect you have in mind—and have fun doing it! The following ideas, hints, and materials will help you in working with your CUT & COPY project:

- a good bottle of white-out—to delete any part of the design that doesn't apply.
- a photo-blue pencil—to draw in items before darkening the lines with a black marker or pen. A photo-blue pencil works much better than a regular pencil.
- rubber cement or removable tape—to mount the different designs together on your working page. This allows you to move the picture around if you need to.
- a fine-tip black marker—to add extra little doodles around the designs you will be putting together.
- a reputable copy shop—to make sure that you will be pleased with the finished product. Find a shop with good machines, because your project will turn out only as good as the copier you use.

To keep this book intact for future use, make sure you work from photocopies of the original illustrations. Enjoy yourself, and may all of your copies turn out wonderful!

© 1993 Dianne J. Hook

ISBN 0-87579-703-2

Printed in the United States of America
10 9 8 7 6 5 4 3 2

Reverence

my family is forever!

Families are forever!

FAMILIES ARE FOREVER!

I AM A CHILD OF GOD

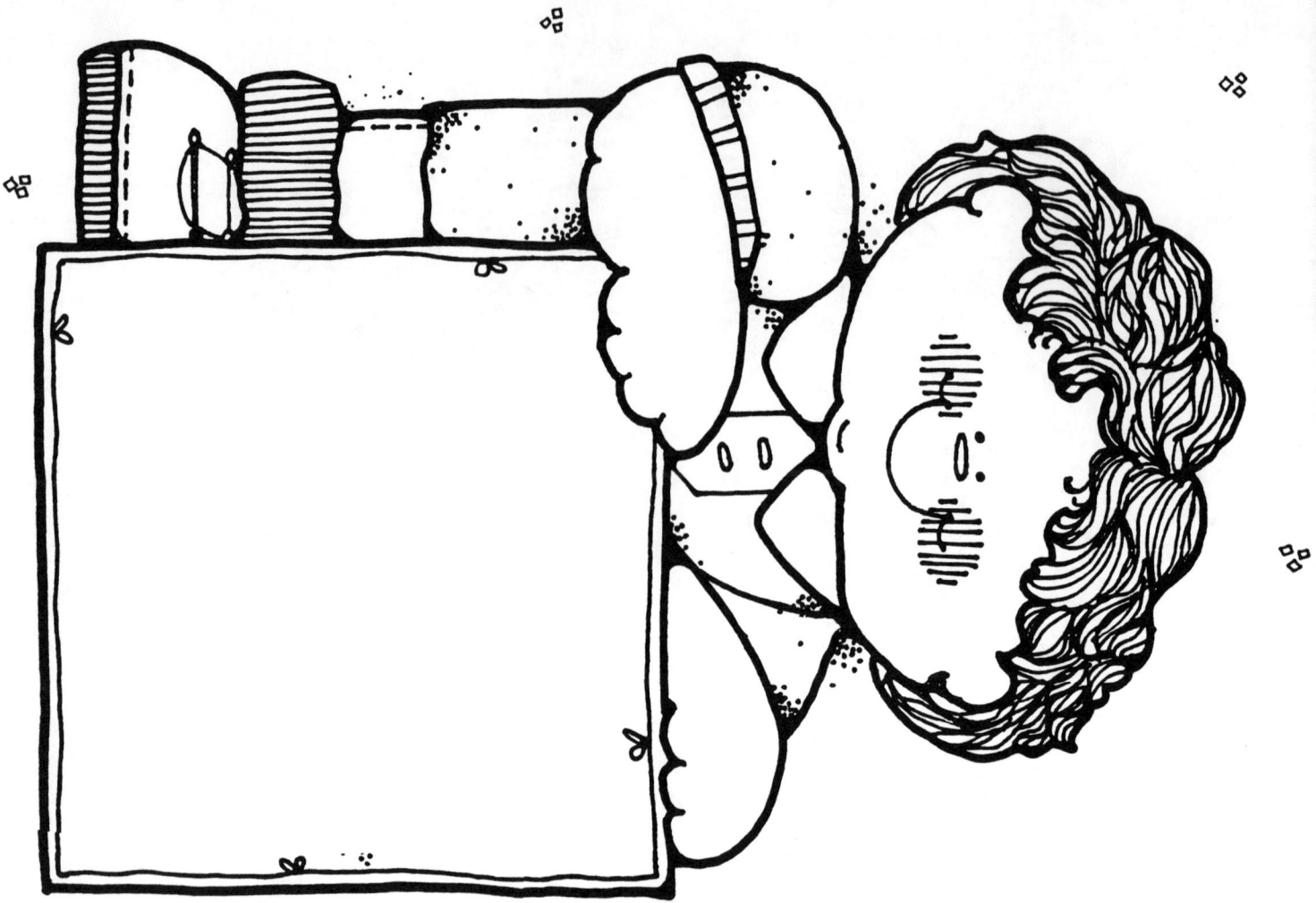

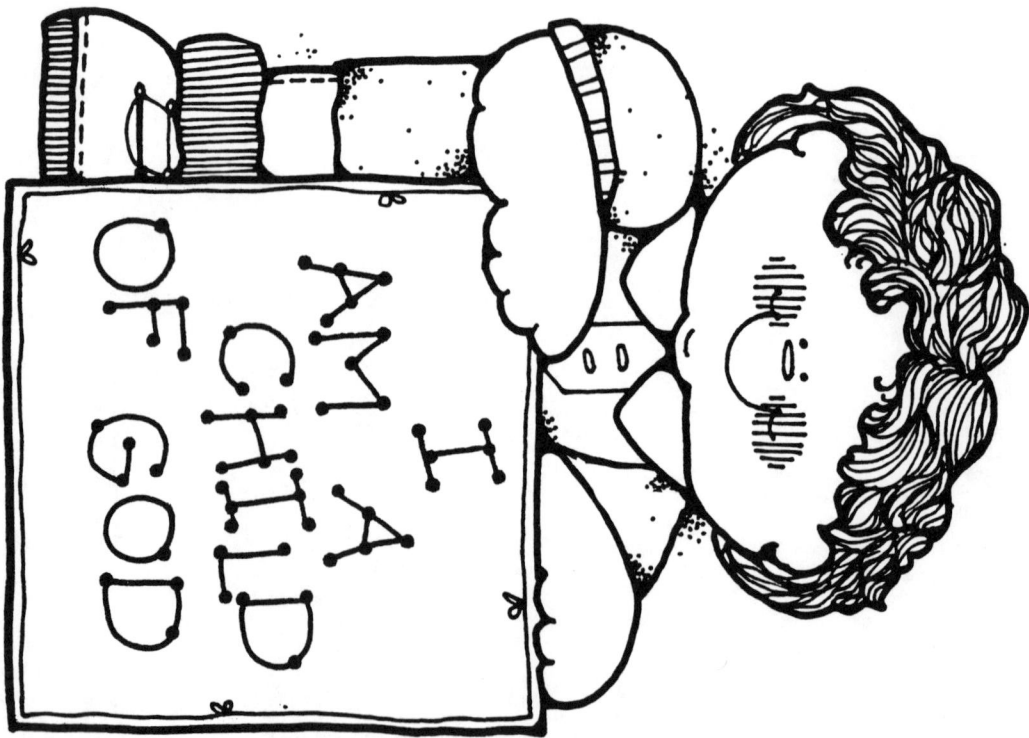

I AM A CHILD OF GOD

PRIMARY

PRIMARY

PRIMARY

PRIMARY

PRIMARY

THANK YOU

from the Primary !

fold
fold

MUSIC

Look who's helping in Singing time.

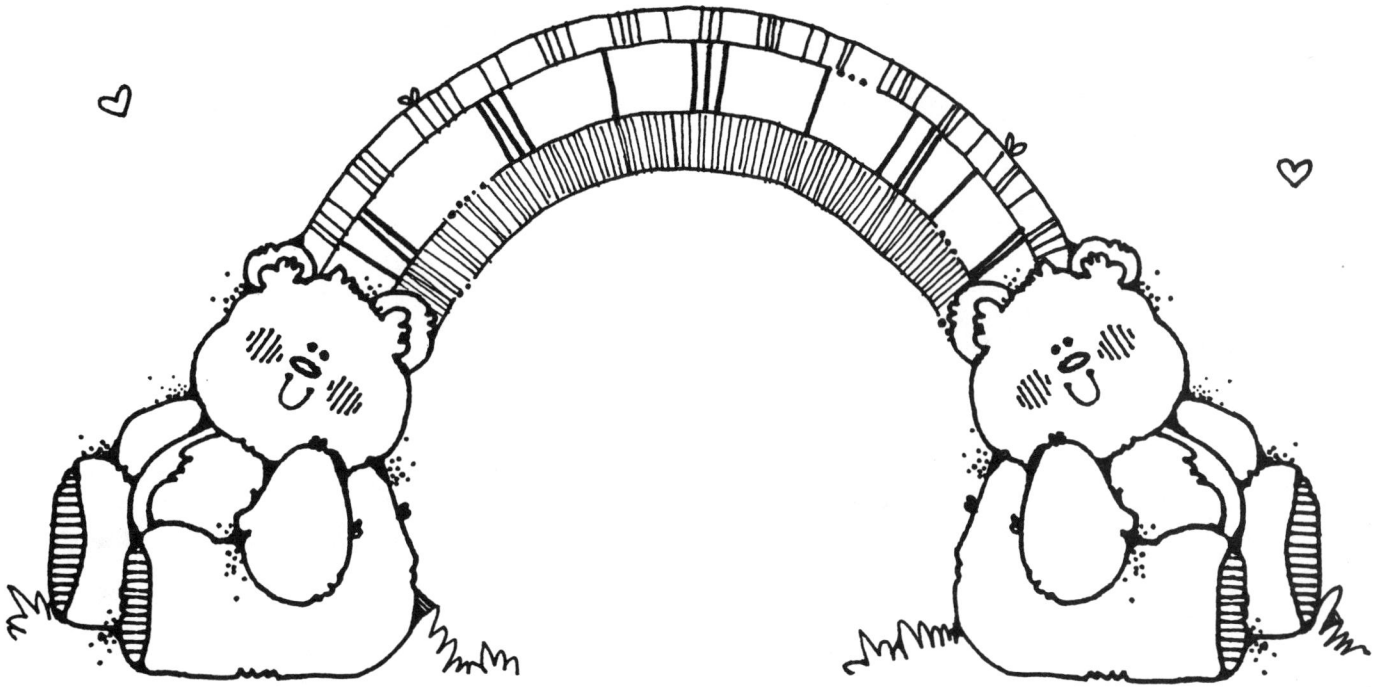

Jesus Wants Me To Be Happy!

Nursery

Primary Activity

Date:

Time:

Place to meet:

With love
From your primary
teacher

With love
From your primary
teacher

I ♥ primary!

We miss you!

Thanks for your help today!

fold — —— fold

from the Primary

Primary
makes
me
happy!

DOGGONE GREAT!

Happy Birthday !

To:

From:

best birthday wishes from the primary presidency !

BIRTHDAY TIME !

Don't miss this!

JUST PAWSING '99

Primary News

a little reminder...

YOU WERE GREAT TODAY!

it's time!

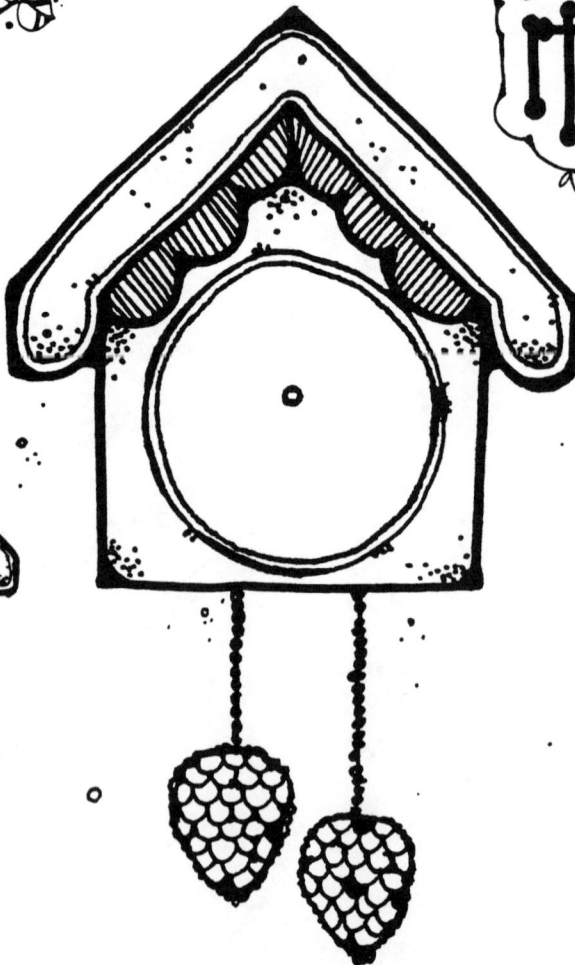
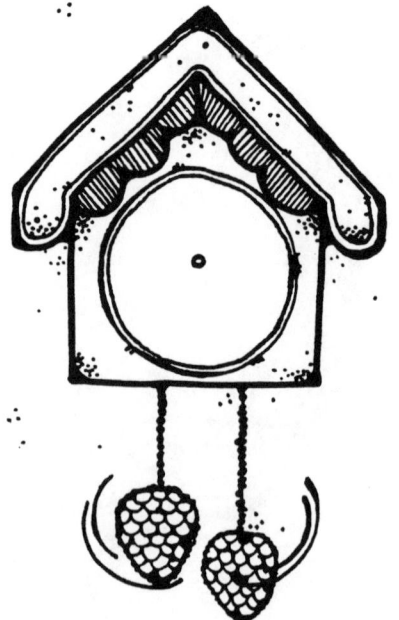

"Stick" to it!

Feed my
Sheep...

Feed my
Sheep...

Read the Scriptures

Read the Scriptures

Bible

Book of Mormon

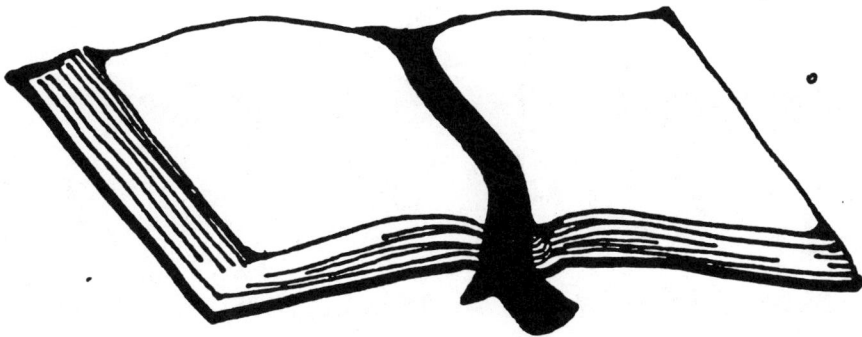

Bible

Book of Mormon

a little reminder...

a little reminder...

Don't Forget

Don't Forget !

name

will be giving a prayer during Sharing Time on

_____

if you have any questions...call...

_____

Don't Forget !

name

will be giving a scripture during Sharing Time on

_____
date

if you have any questions...call...

_____